HOOK

THE HUGH MACLENNAN POETRY SERIES

Editors: Allan Hepburn and Carolyn Smart

TITLES IN THE SERIES

hook

nancy viva davis halifax

McGill-Queen's University Press
Montreal & Kingston • London • Chicago

© nancy viva davis halifax 2015
ISBN 978-0-7735-4580-9 (paper)
ISBN 978-0-7735-9746-4 (ePDF)
ISBN 978-0-7735-9747-1 (ePUB)

Legal deposit third quarter 2015
Bibliothèque nationale du Québec

Printed in Canada on acid-free paper that is 100% ancient forest
free (100% post-consumer recycled), processed chlorine free

McGill-Queen's University Press acknowledges the support
of the Canada Council for the Arts for our publishing
program. We also acknowledge the financial support of the
Government of Canada through the Canada Book Fund
for our publishing activities.

Library and Archives Canada Cataloguing in Publication

Davis Halifax, Nancy Viva, 1956–, author
    Hook/Nancy Viva Davis Halifax.

    (The Hugh MacLennan poetry series)
    Poems.
    Issued in print and electronic formats.
    ISBN 978-0-7735-4580-9 (pbk.).
    ISBN 978-0-7735-9746-4 (ePDF).
    ISBN 978-0-7735-9747-1 (ePUB)

    I. Title. II. Series: Hugh MacLennan poetry series

PS8607.A957H66 2015   c811'.6   c2015-902967-8
                                      c2015-902968-6

This book was typeset by Interscript in 9.5/13 New Baskerville.

CONTENTS

HOOK

INDEX

The founding fathers of Canada   how am I part of this

the recording secretary   speak plainly

Queen Victoria   landscape of empire
the crown   hurt

William Booth   gadding about, no it is
preoccupation and lack of sleep

a chaplain   my answer avoids the full
significance of your question
about this current campaign

Lotte,   Narissa,   we are neither straight nor
Betty,   Valerie,   Marge,   simple but crooked and
Gwin,   Rita,   Kandi,   contrary in our state. We
Marnie   & Sahs,   are often poorly and find
Margrit,   the evidence of our true
Krysta and   existence easily denied

shelter workers, Margrit, Maude   ask only that they are less
extravagant in their daily diet
and unbroken obsessions

the dead   a palimpsest

pigeons   homing, messenger

The sky startles over the intersection.
Pigeons wheel from birds of prey.
Ninety-one women in shared rooms,
as if they were curs –
wetted with the inclemency of mid-day mid-November –

CHAIN II

No longer a hotel   the building
                    has a mission   deliverance
          and prayer
three squares
line ups   medicine
              holy   communion.

She sews shifts from old white linens
cuts her pattern on a round wood table
uses every piece of a plain domestic that was

once tugged across the breadth of faithful and false beds,
laid along lengths of bodies with
unabated longing for washing machine, iron.

She rescued these threads with her scissors
cut themselves into her
necessary. Her hands stare,

paired dizzying trembles thump
the wood table crimson   sheets
splintered from beds and laundry baskets.

INTAKE

A bed under stars, metal stairs,
a concrete coronet, a corner that curves.

The exchange proffered is   a sticky trap :
a new hoodie   grey   a bit large.

NOT AS IMPORTANT AS

These bodies – woven
together, wanted and unwanted,
said and unsaid.

bedbugs, charity, cockroaches, cooks, counselors,
cleaners, chaplains, insecticide, judgments, maintenance,
crews, lice, mice, pity, poison, sin, spare change, used

These bodies –
grown from seed
conceived along terrestrial longitude
speak from east to west
their waiting shapes shimmer

in pulsebeats

in the name of ...

"Well, they are liars."

USES OF THE DEAD

The ropes tether the freshly
risen corpse

for saw and cleaving.
Freed from flesh and sound,

from lively breath,
the ropes are wound

round the cadaver's hand.
Hold still sweet, the ropes command.

And where is your heart,
and where is your lung,

and where is your kidney.
and where is your brain,

and where is your tongue,
and where is your soul,

and where is God
to sew cut skin,

to admit this departure,
to untie this rope?

Men wrecked on the bow of Nature
        mime angels in the eloquence of their bleating.

Ashes of unchronicled hunger fall as lightning clothes
        homes in flame.

Holy water replaced by
        plagues and sins and riots and wives

with golden rings to pawn.
        Waters and dust and rocks agitate panic.

Modest death crawls roped to innocence and guilt
        thankful for transport.

INDUSTRY

How long 'til she slides under?
        Half asleep she plumbs fog

lace. Soap bubbles burst
        over waters of laundry tubs where

she washes night's blossoming
        in this forgetting

place. She is near drowning. She knows,
        a creek once ran to the lake. It was

buried by men who dug 'til they were
        bones and shabby cloth.

She yields to its current:

      Vaughn Road   big mouth bass   Dufferin

northern pike

          brown bullhead

                  Christie

                   pumpkinseed

    Bellwoods

               white sucker

My invocation raises   thoughts

   crumbs of language
     once trapped within dense bone

take flight   pinion
   round the bounds of sea and heaven.

My pen presses   paper's grain.

   Once upon a time, I wrote

        something

    like   laughter.

THE ARMY MARCHES INTO CANADA,
C. 1882

Daughters, mothers, and sisters loiter on morning
  sidewalks.
One, seated with cigarette, slippers, and housecoat
Rests her foot upon her belongings
As if the whole world were her home

One, seated with cigarette, slippers, and housecoat
Last night she slept with William Booth
As if the whole world were his home
His long beard tangles her hair

Last night she slept with William Booth,
One in hope and doctrine, one in charity
His long beard tangles her hair
Him singing

One in hope and doctrine, one in charity
Holy soldier of Christ
Him singing
While resurrection men hurry to death

As if the whole world were their home.

You make soup never
forgetting –

potatoes planted,
two weeks after a hard frost
eyes open facing heaven,
during the dark of the milk moon,
tucked under hills of earth
the ground of Rembrandt's *Juno*,
brown ochre burnt
sienna sepia

– the taste of
sunwarm soil.

LOTTE

I was born in 1935 –
here I am
digging through concrete
picking bottles, salvaging scrap

as the trees lose their leaves.
My mother arrives to sigh
about the slowness of my trek
'cross this land.

There are days I forget
seventy years have passed,
find my mother smiling,
and I am five. She is whistling
like honey, like a kettle.

the full significance   thirty-nine years   unclaimed
        sentimentality

        change   averages   expectancy   statistics

                                dangerous   ~~save~~
safe

                                                                streets
episodes   occupied   empty   discussion   reject

criminal   lost   commonplace   heart   body

do not   ~~talk~~take   life   brutal   expectancy   merciless

Watch these words
brick bandage bridge.
Worry. About side-effects, rabbits,
dogs, the impossibility of understanding.
Be scared. Write

down your questions.
Count church steeples, cash stores.
Do not linger behind the line
or grow impatient.
Be wary of teetering,

trembling, a forward
promise of cure.
Wonder. Know on the other side of the line
women lose consonants to
shallow rattles.

Wait. Watch how ears catch tenor
choral movements, how the tremor of
muscle spills blue and yellow from
white waxed paper cups onto palms.
Watch fingers with hangnails toss pills back dry.

DOUBLE LOVE-KNOT

Walk in.
I am not the couch from your living room,
your nest, or castle. Instead of linen union,
covered in afternoon's west sun
my bright piss yellow –
covers bruised plaster –
bears hunger for raspberry,
a blink of tears, the early years
in the middle of elder decline,
branches of trying times –
tributes. None mean to leave this scrabble.
Their letters settle into my seams
riddles, rules, virtuous policies,
wild decline. They leave
cats' purrs, embroidered cloth, porcelain creamers
in exchange for 3.5 metres.

"Me, I'm gone. Nothing but trouble."
Too many questions
pesky, short, hefty, hairy.

My delicious paintings
fat with colour and beads.
Never quite enough they had a donation

just after I left.
There was cake too. Chocolate with vanilla icing.
I wanted a celebration – it was my birthday

every mouthful of cake singing me – every
brushstroke a history, an angle
my neck straining against the weight.

BETTY

The police
    perform their owl watch
        secure me inside this sleek coop.
                                Cops calculate
        criminals   flower
    in alleys
                a multitude
        drawn to my commemorative plates of
                popes and flowers.   Gold rims
        a dusty accumulation
    buttons and keys.
You
        don't
    believe
                this unsheathed knife.
        Wade through
        my snug dreams
            sell yourself.

VALERIE

Somewhere a woman is walking up steps
in too small shoes
her head down, always
down so you won't catch her eye.

She claims the rocks she stares at in the concrete
certain they're the ones she danced on at Chaleur Beach
her hand in her mother's, two figures against a downwelling
    light.

If only she were here now and not caught some far where
like the way the heel of this damn shoe catches in the step.
And her wrist catches in razors and her
stomach catches pills and booze.

She is setting. Walks with her head down,
her feet in rocks. You can see her any day
walking the stairs with her downward watch,
the rocks blazing.

MARGRIT

How does my desire within these twelve hours
condense as if this nave and its aisles

observe my watch of setting to rising?
Blessings, soap and soup,

hot tea, carefully placed
salvation and nothing changes

and nothing changes.
At night sing beds full

check surveillance footage
for stragglers, for sin

for what is inside her
is what is inside.

The first lesson
do not open the door.

I think about the rough creature
that I cradle, an ill-considered sort of

homely dog with bloodied snout, blistered skin
hanging dull green

who like me has bones and breath and death
who like me is cut and redrawn.

We nip and howl and scratch at our ruin
we rage against pills, half-lives and cocktail

dresses. My medicines are not a gift
that arrive once a year wrapped in transparent tissue

the colour of autumnal grass.
They are needles used to stitch a frock

Drop-waisted brocade with pearls for camouflage.
My medicines present an unflinching threat

if I do not swallow
under their hammers

the promise of recovery will be rescinded.
I wait at the prescription counter for my bottles and boxes

thinking this is how we are,
my beast panting in my arms,

me in a dress,
looking back over rail lines

watching new blades shoot
through earth.

THE CHAPLAIN

The chaplain with her newly shorn head, a second daughter
with a rivalrous past and short nails
smiles at her women, her lost souls.

At night she dreams of pregnancy and rebirth
Leviathan in Lake Ontario
ninety-one sublime women in her choir
on the precipice of orange earth
from their mouths blue frogs with
fine crocheted lace wings grumble
while she trembles at this monstrous revival
ribboned 'cross stream and sky.

Awakes to a chorus:

> O sisters, who art now dead –
> perished by tinned tuna & powdered milk
> by the charity of gamblers and the bounty
> of liquor store donation boxes, by the
> casual language of mathematical calculation –
> I pray you : show mercy.

She brings thirty hats, flowers,
feathers, glitter, glue, balloons
to decorate, to wear while watching
the Royal Wedding

Five-thirty a.m. the television turns from black to faery
the pageantry draws women from their rooms
some still in pyjamas
wear their majesty

declaring something old,
something borrowed
is nothing
new.

She stares at the women
drowning – ivory silk, white lace –
under the goodness of her vocation
a truth hid behind the bosom

of salvation. Wreathes hang
over the entrance to this
sacred garden where wine demonstrates
it was water before

it was grape.
Later, in waiting,
it will be blood. Crimson
stained taste of

mildew, pepper, tobacco,
cedar, the common soldiers
in this army.
One of the women

forgets beauty, curses her age
the certainty of rotting teeth and
heart troubles sealed with
faith in the Kingdom.

Outside, roses climb
a frame of coat hangers
still in their winter
woolens.

MARGE

I took the bus   north   'til scrub and tangled brush   forgot
          the road.   I walked what I could
          mind under sun listening
                                    rustling of brown thrashers.
                    I journeyed
     to leave linoleum-tiled stairs,
                    rusted metal struts, concrete.
          I walked
back   to the mothers: bear, raccoon, snake.
          I left   the city   where earth
            is named dirt where
          a weed is swept   from stoop into sewer-belly's current.
I slept.   My bed   sheeted with   partridge berry,
          whorled wood   aster,   trout lily.
I left the city,   where nothing seeded   came
to flower.
          North

                              to   the mothers.

I run toward her arms
open. Celeste's at the back of the line,
defying celestial mechanics
dressed in layers of shirts and sweaters, carrying

three bags, I grab one.
Our waiting is dogged by history,
mass forms a shore line
herring gulls drop crabs on rock.

We catch up.
Standard assumptions.
Maintain without offence
a scratching and bleating.

Her mouth's burning, she's lost time,
gained weight. She says "Hands have a geometry,
they calculate the width of their bite."
Meaning's been confiscated by metabolites.

She's earned one of the humbler
bodies which daily endurance orbits.
The impress of her cure
logged in

how-to and how-not-to books
is a weak force that cannot still her line,
her attraction and the resistance of air.
All objects fall the same way.

A LIFE COMPOSED, AGE THIRTEEN

Awkward child, arms and legs angled
to catch every bruise thrown.
readied by cigarettes at ten
she finds a place behind a door
where her frame's slight strength
is shored up.
Her copper hair
less bright than the
flame held under a spoon, where
she cooks and washes.

Other children held close behind doors
their light framed by curtains and locks and homework.
Smoke rings drift from her lips,
sometimes she falls asleep
burning. Awake, her mouth opens to filch
the last touch of relentless dark.
Later breathes it out,
exhales a lawn, two trees, a row of bushes.
Witch, criminal, mad girl, dreamer,
lover, she is
framed by dark
relentless
exhalations.

BUTTERFLY STITCH

Behind her eyes the world inverts.
One cheek bruised, her violet eye half shut.
No one recognizes her,
no baker hands her coffee and sweets.

She looks toward windows
lit by early morning.
The street's darkness welcomes this paned rescue.
100 years ago this corner, forest.

Sugar maples, their skins thick and smooth
too slow, they stood smelling the tar,
watching the burn.
Not thinking.

HOUSE

She surveils the landscape
knowing that as sure as she'd scratch an itch
she would change the size of everything.

Finding nothing fit was not a surprise, nor were
tatty red fabric chairs. New covers, matching pillows
would be necessary.

She could easily
persuade the women into the chamber
with tea, cookies, and a bit of yarn.

They wouldn't cut the laws from their
old patterns, they'd freestyle something
for the resizing.

EACH BODY REMEMBERS THE NECESSARY DISTANCE BETWEEN BEDS

"75 cm" in case of emergency.
Which disaster are we rehearsing?

Heads down, tucked into curled necks.
think fiddleheads, spiral of

growth, pin
cushions, the air prickling.

HOOK

I grab a hook.
*Let one end of the yarn cross over its other, fold it under,
pull it through the centre gently, loopily.
Take my hook and insert it into that first loop and pull it
   tight ...

Chain 2. Have a sip of tea. Look up, breathe out.

Take my hook and draw the yarn over,
close to the catch in the hook
duck the yarn through the chain on the hook.
Make another.

Repeat: yarn over, duck the yarn.

Gaunt women   With A, ch 5.
         fat women, join with sl st
                  crippled women, chain 3 sts blind
women, 8 trc in ring   dead women,   join w sl st
look toward a bronze statue and its open mouth
waiting for her to sing 16 dc in ring

A small bird perches with B, ch 3
on her bottom lip, 2 dc in next dc
ch1, turn. Sc in same st. Skip 2 sts, dc 6 in next st. Skip 2 sts,
   sc in
next st. Repeat from *

She turned on the tap,
filled her bucket, and
sloshed it across the floor
yellow gloves half way to her elbows,
singing Johnny, singing Anita's "Ring of Fire"
she scoured walls, ceramic tile floors, cupboards.
Poured boiling water into the bone
china cup with the shepherd girl.
Pulled her kitchen chair to the window.
Elbows on the sill, she drank sweet tea.
Listened: nighthawks.

Like I had to leave the shelter … I got a room in this really big really old house … no locks on the doors … then I had to f'kn leave that place … middle of the night in the Coffee Time some man lent me his phone … my stuff my drawings and pens and shit. fk. … still there …but I got another room … I'm gonna move today … no lock on the door. … so I go in and out through the window, leave a chair under the doorknob. a knife in the doorframe … no big deal …

SOS

SOS

plz

MARNIE & SAHS

I never hid my thoughts.
I sat opposite her and we'd both
look into the bit of blue tunnel
that we could see through her window.

I knew she never wanted to leave
this room overlooking the deserted
No Frills parking lot.
She told me it fit like her last eviction.

I brought grapes to share and she said she wouldn't eat
anything the colour of running sores or rotting fish.
Lately she's glimpsed blackened red and wants brightness,
light that splits clouds

like skin pulled taut over
a skein of bones. Maybe, she says, she's seen a scraggly man
with a whiskered jaw,
who is not the god who

threads hell's screws, no, no, he's the other one, named
Dreadful, who screams us all awake,
who culls sleep to ship to
distant provinces.

Even before she told me that
I knew she wasn't sleeping. At night I heard her
snarling as she did mathematical calculations
in French, I heard the chittering of bedbugs who
watched over the one and two and three a.m. of us.
She knows we're good, she's forever
lodged in my heart, like betrayal, a lit cigarette,
a dead weight in fading light.

OLD HOTEL

My desire for beauty, not yet pressed,
shares its ambition:
to that one I say wash your hands, wash your weepy flesh.
She walked my stairs until, ruined, I let her out

scolding her wash your hands, your weepy flesh
lest red smells of old blood stains. To that one –
her wearing borrowed clothes
good enough for wearing to the

Coffee Time at the five corners
I say don't be scared. Her fears
freed in my newly skinned room
tremble under sheets and

that one ever unloved I would
confine in the emptiest of four
doubled bunks, sweet cinnamon, snatchin'
at my limin awkward full.

KRYSTA

I thirst for vision not some damn cheap shadow
    Give me doubled headbanging

        darkness   The view from this black
life blessings from the   poor   You think

      of us as ageing whores As
lost souls in need of salvation But I'd never

pawn this for Your pearls or your
               Jesus view of heaven.

In this life you may be harnessed to a Mortgage   ($1,453)
dignify the choice of Dior through
conversations on social relations
hold celebrated dinner parties   ($459)

classify your choice of debt as a
misunderstanding a promise of securities you maintain
your celebrated dinner parties with cake
your accumulation of regret   ($1,453)

the purchase of secure promises understanding
your ruin is welcomed by instant approval, 2% savings
as your accumulation of regret   ($2,954)
echoes, murmurs cracks provoke a crumbling

leaks reversed by instant approval, 2% savings
you conceive of possessions imagine a home
your accumulation of regret   ($5,492)
the ways of plumbing the taste of cake

you conceive of a home imagine possessions
hold celebrated dinner parties   ($9,245)
devoid of the language of plumbing the taste of cake
In this life harnessed to a Mortgage

you may be ruined you may imagine   ($15,739)

HOMES

a frame American colonial
hall and parlour
Spanish colonial backsplit
barraca barracks
barndominium bay
and gable basement
bungalow bedsit
brownstone Cape
Cod cape
dutch castle chalet chattel
house cottage
American
craftsman deck
dogtrot
duplex earth
sheltered estate
farm faux chateau
federal front
split foursquare French
colonial gab lefront gambrel
garden garrison
geodesic Georgian
halfway houseboat
Izba Konak log long
loft lustron manor
mansion maisonette

mediterranean mcmansion

mews micro mission

mobile modern

monolithic Monterey

mud sod octagon

pent rooming

row palace

pole poor prairie prefabricated

pueblo Queen Anne

queenslander ranch

roundhouse row

saltbox splitlevel

stick Sears

catalog shack

shotgun detached single

souterrain southern Spanish

colonial Spanish

revival stilt

snout storybook

tenement terraced

tree Tudor

Victorian villa

wealden wimpey

workhouse

ROOMMATE

I offered you my prettiest handkerchief but you say "not
now" – "before I leave." You won't remember your promise.

If you do it's not 'til a week or more after. Leaving for you
was a kind of fasting. I determine to imagine "not now"

as a ghost, and "before I leave" like the bus that misses my
stop. The abandoned hankie returns to my drawer

where a bag of lavender dried by August sun releases its
near-transparent scent. You'd been here since

February, arriving with the blistering cold. Or maybe it was
March, that week we lost winter. The week you'd given me

the word "mango." A yellow word with a southerly shape, a
lip like wind. The clumsiness of "handkerchief" now so

obviously a mistake, I hunker down on the curb, thinking
about the tongue as a cross, a gaudy muscle.

HEADLINES

The morning newspaper
stacks stories,
death has been domesticated.
Misery is hollow bones
blanketed in headlined tragedy,
murder, famine, extinction.

At work, I don't lift my head. Shove my
hands into cheap plastic,
smear plastic cheese
white bread with a plastic knife.
Just the right amount. Smile.

Push the elevator buttons. Signs
inside command self-control: press once.
Surveillance cameras watch. fk you. Push
once, three, four, five, eleven times 'til
at last the clattering
jaws close.

Read the sign over the peanuts.
For a dollar I can add to some campaign.
And eat.

The children I seen are fighters and lovers
all of 'em. Half are dead or half toward.
Some in jail. For sure one burned,
that was my brother.

But tonight in fine form
dancing in this one bright spot,
don't they strut in
like small-town criminals
stealing words too long left in pockets.

Her hunger clocks
the sun's rise
embers breathe
fog. Her dream lingers
three metres from the highway
hot coffee laid on
gingham, toast and fruit.
Sweet filled
cars squint
into the morning.
She holds out her thumb,
       going some far where.

A LIFE COMPOSED, AGE ELEVEN

At eleven she began to take control
knowing the consequences on her slight frame,
        like a bedtime story.

Locked in, she opened
the window, jumped
        to the picnic table, scampered like

one of the Flopsy Bunnies. Hiding in bushes
she watched the car lights until they disappeared,
        then to the next bush.

A LIFE COMPOSED, AGE TWELVE

The heat of estrogen startles them.
At twelve the daughter burns.
The mother, perimenopausal, has had her fill.
Her daily affirmations spoken into the mirror,
reflected back as shrieked accusations.
The fecundity is too much. Father,
resorts to fists and drinking to tame the girl

who lopes off to hills to be with her pack.
Living in woods, at the edges of fields, sleeping
under signs on highways.
In boxcars they raise each other up.

Old man, who works at the bottling plant,
thinks the way she rounds the corner at thirteen is beautiful.
He lets her and a friend sleep together
in a single bed in his walk-up flat.
feeds them white bread, Cheez Whiz, and Coke.
In stores pale orange tomatoes in cellophane packages
find their way into coats.
The shopkeepers extend
kindness toward hungry girls.

The guy who owns the pool hall lets her
vacuum tables after hours
she picks up
tricks to keep safe.
A few brothers accumulate
love and hate tattooed on knuckles, so cool.
Make a family to live
in the woods. The church choir is distant.
The dream of a father and mother
is quit.

WHAT TO DO IF YOUR COUNTRY
STOPS BREATHING

Hold her in your arms.

Call her   best friend
while you gather courage
        to breathe
                small breaths into rivers   compress

                hills,   two   three

Call her thirty-six fathers from the grave.

APPROACHING SORROW

While I sleep
the memorial to the homeless dead sleeps
harnessed to an injury

of names (johndoejuanitadoejohndoejohn
doejuandoejohndoejohndoejanedoejohn
doejane). Under the heat of yellow linen

sweat stitched by needle workers
I dream an alphabet –
names of men, closed doors,

acts of violence
in legislative houses. Gyrating
maple keys navigate

ground and water,
emerald lawns chafe under
silent alarms.

SHE WAITED

She waited on the eastern sea-to-sea-
to-sea tracing men trundling past
carts barren of bottles or copper or fish
hands roughed by minus seventeen with wind
jackets un-ironed coarse cotton.

She waved to skies, clouds
in their gauzy pink rising shine tasted
like candy streams. Her hands wore scars
illuminated in sun's golden set:
one from gutting fish, another
a broken glass hidden in sudsy dish water,

a corrupt grease trap.
She missed her kids. Hoped the sweaters she
knit still fit, were not worn
through. She was saving up a story to tell them why
she had to leave, why

they were taken, but she couldn't get beyond
once upon a time without biting
her nails to the quick, without thinking
she should be able to clean up this mess of a
life where the shape of the future is ferried
from harbours passed.

THIS CUP IS THAT COLOUR

I heard her   voice
laced with Ursa Major
Do you have coffee?
sorry – tea   powdered milk   white sugar
that's it.

Guess I'll take this one
its colour reminds me of a car I had   had
a hole in the floor
and the window on the driver's side stuck
but once I saw a great blue heron from that window.

Sometimes the forest grew
right up to the tarmac tried to come
in through the window the car filled with rustley green
crushed shad flies
until it was all gassed out we'd drive and Ger would suggest
    siphoning
but I'd rather walk to the station and bum ten bucks worth.

We slept in that car
the cold coming in from that stuck window
hiding in an alley or parking lot
we'd watch the moon come out from under the clouds covers
pulled up to our noses we'd sing songs
in tune with nighthawks
'til dawn and cops knocked and cats retreated.

This cup is that colour.

CURBSIDE

winterboots with holes a bit small two t-shirts that are green
cross stitch picture from mom a drawing that shar gave me
four markers a sweater that fits good my diary a floral curtain
for a kitchen science fiction book third in a series a purse
from the sally sewing bits straight pins a sock puppet that my
niece made bin bags heritage seeds I think forget-me-nots an
ancient church cookbook maps of places to visit towels hand
soap empty cloth bags an umbrella in case of rain tin of soup
plastic spoons forks extension cord acorns string teabags

These gifts given curbside
reveal time's fade,
time's worn gaze.
This world's time of sloppy grinding decay,
the blackgreen boreal forest coloured bag's drape.
Its modest obscenity. Its metallocenic virtuosity.

BLUEPRINT

Time fades.   Soiled petticoats dry in cold rooms.   No Vacancy signs.
   Hunger moons reflect in amber
lights. You wonder if this old hotel is where surrender gathers her seeds.

  You wait, sitting, listen to Beverley's careful measure.
    Drag your plate over the stain on the
   tablecloth.
   Watch handprints gather   at the exit,

  watch the stain on the wall.   Strain toward
   spilled tattles.
    Go for a smoke,   answers.

THE APPEARANCE OF IMPROBABLE
CONTINGENCIES

See her?
Steadfast and firm her
branches graze the mantle of quiet clouds
as she elaborates her claim

on concrete. What are we –
all who walk past?
See her?
Arms creak'n with damp

memories.
Steamy days
rabbles of bluebottles,
her singing

neighbours.
Mark her
before twenty-five cents above
becomes a trap.

PINEAPPLE PATTERN

Veiled by hook and half hidden
the pale strength of an insect

survives the loop and clumsily flies off to the interior of my
    souvenir teacup.
My hands work one stitch one stitch one stitch,

'til a surface is strung from cotton strands.
A fine lace woven each day as a watch.

Imagine, this way of marking time (one scarf, two mittens,
    a sweater)
each knot a tick or tock,

each row an hour,
and evening is when we cast off,

unwind the skein –
As my hand lifts your night –

our past hours, worn,
we turn once again.

LULLABY — GARDINER EXPRESSWAY

Goodnight street
Good night fear
Good night bedbugs knitting me mittens
Good night fight
And the boy getting f'cked thirty feet from me

Goodnight rats
Goodnight muck
Goodnight feral cats
And goodnight to the parking lot
where men in their cars
scratch their heads as they explode
their dicks laying limply on their laps.
their empires far up their own arses
on a good night

Good night cocks
And goodnight cops
Goodnight ya little shit
And goodnight to the protracted
fck'n suffering of daily lack

Goodnight broken arm
And goodnight hunger

Good night love

Good night dry socks
And goodnight to all of us of imperfect nature with
unknown f'kn purpose.

Good night to friends, the beloved dead
Good night charity
Good night wretches everywhere.

Information tells us little that is useful:
fourteen nights
eighty-two beds
seven women
forty years
three thousand
thirty-nine years.

Do not imagine gathered facts as complete sets.
A fact is ill-equipped
language starved
does not sing the bone curve of pine
has never stooped to hear grass
had no illiterate childhood.

Normed and damned – ill-equipped,
ill with reason. Equipped with truth:
seal cubs, the Stanley Cup, the Saskatchewan cobalt bomb –
can never remember the joke's end, the one about
the zamboni, the Newfoundland premier, and the codfish.

CLASSICAL CONDITIONING

Renovation completed,
my sturdy landings smell :
          laundry soap, bleach,
     dry paint

          : miramichi thunder

               : candied ginger

dining hall	binder type
bath	surfactant
kitchen	biocide
entrance way	defoamer
chapel	co-solvent
laundry	thickener
dormitory	dirt resistance

The sound of a metronome
elicits canine

     arousal
          words secrete
          meaning
          and then doubt

          : bruised cherry

          : pixie stix   : mouse back

          : final straw.

too sweet, shallow. the sweat of sugar lines
      her thoughts

      she steadies the needle

her hands

shake   you know she's not
                       stone

can't speak   can't answer
      even supposing things are tender

are chill

            narrow strips of buckram with buckles

      with wheelbarrows and   baskets, gaskets,

       thickets, sprockets
     straight on.   Tell me

when morning shines.

Somewhere. I was going somewhere, probably east.
I was listening to the pattern of wrinkled curtains
listening to shadows fold.
I was going somewhere
remembering the hands of an old woman
the back bench of a bus
maybe the hands of a broken clock.
I was remembering the east
watching the wrinkles of shadows cleave.
I was going somewhere
listening to broken wrinkles, the pattern
of a bus, the folding of
the sun along
her narrowed western edge
drawing lines
cleaving the curtains of
a life with broken beats.
I was probably in the east
walking across fog-drenched sand
going somewhere for a broken clock.
Somewhere I was listening to
a clatter of shadows
a wrinkle of clouds
flinch across the eastern horizon.

FARE

She gets on.
     She needed to get but she
         didn't have 3 bucks she had
             cops behind grasping at
                her getting and

             the driver – 4 days on the job and here
        this woman
      could be his sister
    all tangley
hair and fear with

lipstick last time heartachey
     hospital gowned on geodon
        he blinks, her whoop
           breaks the surface like she was 5
              easing her toes

into the lake
    he was 7 taking care
      they were watching saturday morning
          cartoons with cereal and
             he blinks, at 17 smokes a cigarette

scent of mustard garlic and
>dogs everywhere his muscles
>>hard enough to split faces she danced
>>>on the waves sure of her sacred nature small
>>>>child hands turned up, each day her chirrup-
>>>>ing servant, and

>>what else is a wave before
>she is pulled under, at 18
he in the water with her breathing and
>>the horses drag them under
>>>he lets go in the white crash of sirens

>>>she is quivering gone, eyes turned to sky
>>>and
>police feet
>>bloodied by dancing churning jerking
on fire always a storm
>>she looks to him

25 years dip below the horizon
>the police
>>the woman
>>>not his

THREE STRIKES

No one ever told me that.   No one.
If they told me   that   that
it was three
               well if they told me that
I would not have been shoved to this curb's shoulder.

The first nudge – I complained. One of the women – turns
out there was something monkeying with her insides so she
could not turn the light off   squaring
off about cudgels and hastening all night   losing
sleep turns out
        she complained.

The second screw,
missed curfew by like five minutes
the worker didn't
understand
we had cracked
the dark and just
one more
buttery vanilla bean
praline
reach mattered.

Last knock, tips me
outta here. I had needle and thread
In my room

and maybe I got mouthy
had a word swap with staff
who found 'em.   That's
the third.

EMERGENCY

It is never casual. The emerged
reek of shrinking time. Cars will not
start, water freezes in pipes,
snow rots wheat, trains filled with

iron ore are swallowed.
Animal notes ascend. An emergency
is not a coincidence, simultaneous
celebration, a circuit of delight.

Its maw curtains the favourited body
stitched with dirt and salt and stone.
Montreal earthquake, Tseax Cone, Quebec bridge collapse,
    Miramichi
fire, Halifax explosion, Springhill mining disaster, Ocean
    Ranger.

Do you have another needle?
I just need a bit more thread.
Can I take these with me?
Do you have a minute?
There is less than an inch left
I just need some help
in sewing up this heart
Can you hang on,
just a sec? I
feel too old for this, I'm
sixty-seven now. These pants don't
fit. Do we have any elastic
just a bit would do? I am
so hungry. Can anyone
spare a token? I didn't sleep
last night. There is nothing wrong
with her heart. I read in the *Guardian*
that his body weight was incompatible
with life. I can show you
how to make a poodle
and if you run out
you can make a clown. They cut
his benefits. I finished that one,
it's really good. Gillie is still waiting
it's been so long, she needs something. Can you
help me? I spilled black pigment

on the floor and my hands ache. I
might be pregnant. I'm tired.
We could write the letters instead, the thank
yous. So tired,
I have the 5 a.m. shift. Last week
she took the nice thing. I just want to stop
for a moment. OH you brought
lemon loaf! Oh my mouth is
watering. So these two
are not the same stitch?
Do you want me to make
a cup of tea?
Would you like
my
juice?
Mint?
It's not what we're supposed to have.
She leans her head down. They are,
yup, them, they're looking. Rosey
rubs her back. She needs a bit more.
Look – wow. So radiant.
Can you teach me?
Can you teach me that stitch?
This one, sure.

PERSISTENCE AT THE THRESHOLD
— LIZAKIM

Wearing a moss stitch white hat
knit knit purl purl Repeat

she slices the unexpected
into apples for sharing

pares the latest confinement
feeds our increase in appetite

ripping strips of yarn
from acrylic hoodies

unravels knots
knits the facts of immiseration :

lace openings, yarn over
(slip slip knit) purl

free crochets the failures of
accounting, spills

boiling water over tea leaves
shows you revolution in the bottom of your cup

hand over hand
teaches her

stitches, patterns
a revival.

74

PRAYER TO PRAYER TO PRAYER (GRACE)

How much their prayers loved
eating rose petals
thin layers between slices of
buttered bread sprinkled with turbinado

sugar. Her prayer, loud
voiced dressed in the
certainty of a cardinal number
counted itself not as praise,

commitment, or a door.
Perched on her shoulder
it told her unearned
relentless disapproval would be

temporary. The appearance of wings
would signal success.
Feeling her back for nubs,
her hand moved

upward touched bone
panic. Hung her head   ·
against the velvet
weight of antler.

It's not that a more pious
prayer was needed,
it's just that hers could
awaken slaughter.

ON MONDAY NIGHT, JENNY

slips onto the couch
spills herself into a cuppa tea.

Exhausted by here here Here and here
I watch her stained fingers smooth

wrinkles on her skirt
touch ear then

teacup, return to skirt,
to hair. No motion stranded.

She plucks out
evidence –

ivory, moon,
drywall, shortbread,

picket fences, bone, maggot –
colours, the tired lines of days.

Never taught how to bear
they get it right by the third
narrowing statistical probabilities is the way we put it
the first two experiments
without controls

double blinded
with ever-smaller margins of error.
The first two

twinned in death
on pavement
mostly beak with ant on lucent body
heel-toed, heel-toed.
The third opens her yellow-limned mouth.

AS I READ WHAT IS OF LESS
AND LESS INTEREST

moments pass.
Backspace, erase, find words that are not
exhausted. In the first part of your day

sprawl along the river
sketch the contour of ear or moustache
draw the perfect disguise until it
finds your face.

Wait on the platform.
Make your shame flakey.
Arrive dressed in mismatched thoughts
and orange tights.
Shred a skein or two slunderously.

THE COMMONS (A CHORUS)

1. I didn't say anything before. No one ever asked about
2. I would like nothing more than friendly relations, finding
3. home as in homebody, as in home sweet home, as in

1. what happened. About what got taken : warmth, dry
2. them essential when one knows so few others and suffers
3. homemade as in whipped butter, as in homesick, home

1. shoes, the fat full moon, staghorn sumac, my porcelain
2. with the paleness of hands, the depth of a callous, an
3. decor, home town, rest home, homey as in homestay

1. creamer, the blue eyes of my little brother. They turned all
2. ecstasy of disclosures, invisible flapping of wings
3. temporary or catastrophic, as in home run, home plate,

1. of it into counts : corn, showers, sleeps. There is something
2. lingering close smells, a stinking hall – I feel awfully alone.
3. homeland, home birth, home spun, as in homestead, as in

1. grey, which strains my tolerance and dampens my appetite.
2. to get on my knees – no – to be raised up – no – just to rest
3. home rule as in glorious glory oh glory true north nation,

1. if they knew they would do something,
2. if they knew they would do something,
3. if they knew they would do something,

1. I had a wildness that was never stripped or regulated –
2. as in home range, home truth, home stretch, as in homburg,
3. homage, homebrew, homicide or even hostile, home

1. wouldn't they?
2. wouldn't they?
3. wouldn't they?

1. and now two slices with a thin skim of cream cheese,
2. and not to have others interfere with my physical
3. wrecker, as in shelters as in malingering, as in cleansed

1. translucent cucumber. This last slice – it is something to
2. sovereignty or try to show me the light. there is nothing
3. hearts, as in the rustling of social conscience. as in

1. write on with butter or tear into crumbs, a morse code or –
2. self-evident here. what about the idea of rescue? is it not
3. homemaker, home work, home grown, homecoming, as in

1. if burnt I can scrape into the burn, inscribe a message.
2. cold and ungenerous? I would rather have retribution.
3. home economics, home fries on saturday mornings,

1. I just need a way to tell. We can't have this no-account
2. if you have doubt about the course I am taking or
3. as in destitution before birth as in

1. do you remember?
2. do you remember?
3. do you remember?

1. ending, separated by gaunt trees and locked doors. Once,
2. require a different arrangement of these cots then you best
3. dreadful misery as in

1. we knew each other : borrowed sugar, drank tea, ate
2. speak plainly and soon. there are events and occurrences
3. meagre bodies that need stitches

1. cookies – we were neighbours. We were neighbours.
2. that have provided me an undignified sweep.
3. as in ever uncelebrated – is there no alternative?

1. We were neighbours – is there no alternative?
2. This scrawny quarter where I am found fills me with
3. do you remember?

1. do you remember?
2. melancholy, the impress of which brings me to a realization
3. do you remember?

1. we knew
2. that my resolution of escape set adrift
3. what happened

1. do you remember?
2. do you remember?
3. do you remember?

ACKNOWLEDGMENTS

These poems were written to address the ongoing extremity of suffering within Canada. These poems were written alongside my experience of witnessing homelessness, poverty, disability, and chronic illness on the streets and within women's emergency shelters in Canada. They are a shabby lot wherein live my historical and contemporary understandings of the politics of poverty, the lack of housing in the Canadian landscape, and the systemic violences sustained by bodies at the margins. The poems do not explain or rationalize these lacks, but present emotional responses – a multiplicity of narrative truths, not facts, through which the poet as witness provides an account. The poems rely on imagination – my imagination and that of the reader. They do not present truths, but fragments found in chance passing. The work is not rational, logical – it lies in a domestic, a plain cloth. It is my hope that in these poems the people and the sites of homelessness become more – they become sites for and of memory with all of its failures.

I would like to acknowledge the women, men, and others who live and die rough in Canada – there is a need for an audience for your lives. There is a need for a cultural response.

To the women who have been and are part of Monday Art Group – I miss you, always.

I am forever grateful to my world-changing daughters who are the heart of all of my work, and to my sister Cynthia whose calls and conversations altered our geographical distance. This manuscript was ragged and unfinished when I first brought it to Jay MillAr and the Long Poem workshop at the Toronto New School of Writing. There my sister poets read and encouraged (with gratitude): Dilys Leman, Sue MacLeod, Beatriz Hausner, Lynn McClory, and Dyan Marie. Many thanks are also directed toward Lorna Crozier at Wintergreen Studio, Priscila Uppal, and Karen Solie at Sage Hill and the many colleagues who sat at those workshop tables. To my dean in the Faculty of Health, Harvey Skinner, gratitude for the Dean's Catalyst Award and a sabbatical, which allowed the time to bring the manuscript to completion. To friends, thanks for evenings of delicious food and reading, Sheila Stewart for tea and reading and writing afternoons, Kim Jackson for being part of Red Wagon and for being my friend. To stan, my ever-present shadow and light who meanders alongside through High Park and beauty. My dear friend and editor Cindy Fujimoto interpreted for me the high-level abstractions of comma, colon, capital. She is kind in her knowledge that these are eternally confusing. Thanks to the wonderfuls of McGill-Queen's: Mark Abley, Carolyn Smart, and Ryan Van Huijstee for support and gentle encouragement.

"A Life Composed, Age Thirteen," "A Life Composed, Age Twelve," and "A Life Composed, Age Eleven" were published in earlier forms in "Writing Inequity and Pursuing Hope: Testimonies and Witnessings from Arts-Informed Research," in *Creative Arts in Interdisciplinary Practice, Inquiries for Hope and Change*, edited by Cheryl McLean and Robert Kelly (*International Journal of the Creative Arts in Interdisciplinary Practice*, 2010).

"Valerie" was published in an earlier form in "Reading Boots, Reading Difference," in *Radical Psychology* 8, no. 1 (2010).

"What Is Said," "Not as Important as," "The Army Marches into Canada, c. 1882," and "The Chaplain" appeared in earlier forms in the *Canadian Journal of Disability Studies* 1, no. 3 (2012).